JOURNALING
TO FINANCIAL FREEDOM

JOURNALING
TO FINANCIAL FREEDOM

By

Angelica Maria

I Am Angelica Maria
www.iamangelicamaria.com

Library of Congress Cataloging in Publication Data
ISBN: 978-0-9988706-1-8

Introduction

If you are reading this book, you were drawn to it for one of two reasons: either you love journaling or you want financial freedom. Both would've grabbed my attention; both still do. I love journaling! I love journals! I have so many that I am not sure I will ever fill all of them before I stop picking up new ones. For me, there is something about putting pen to paper—the smoothness of ink gliding on the paper, thoughts streaming out of my mind, being able to see my stream of consciousness alive. I love it! And financial freedom is always at the forefront of my mind. It is the purpose of my business, the focus I bring to my clients, and a personal goal of my own.

With today's electronic world, we spend so much time typing, texting, voice-recording, that we often rarely write. We track our ideas, dreams, thoughts, and goals using pictures or apps in our phones, lists, or quick voice memos. Our phone and tablets have turned into one-stop shops for everything. I am going to tell you that this is not a way to success. In *Think and Grow Rich,* Napoleon Hill continuously reiterates: "make your desires clear and put them in writing." He even recommends reading them out loud to reinforce the belief in your own mind. Your mind has to focus. Your goals and dreams need to be concrete and real. And they need to be written down.

Financial freedom may also be a goal or dream of yours, which may be why you picked up this book. Many people strive for this all of their lives. Some people achieve it by working hard, focusing, and being diligent. Others get a lucky break that leads them to their financial freedom. Some are still striving. If you are reading this, you are most likely in the last category. You want more out of life; you don't want to have to worry about bills or money anymore; you want more than enough money to live life the way you would want to! THAT is financial freedom, right?? You HAVE more than enough money. You are financially secure.

Throughout my life, I was always drawn to both. I wrote this book because I know the journey. I know the struggle and the desire to be financially free. I am writing this book because I have a strong desire to help others. I have a strong desire to help others heal. In this case, my desire is to help you reach your money and financial goals. I have a strong desire to help you heal your money mindset. I have a strong desire to help you reach financial freedom.

Here is the real question: Do you have a strong enough desire to do the work in this book? Do you have a strong enough desire to finish the book? Do you have a strong enough desire to be honest, to do the journaling, to really look at your situation, and to make the changes? Because if you truly want financial freedom, that is what you are going to have to do. You'll need to put in the time and the energy to complete this journey. You'll need to be honest with yourself. You'll need to also get all of that stuff that's in your head out—mental chatter, old beliefs, negative thoughts. That's why we journal!

On this journey, you may find it helpful to have someone with you. Grab a friend, a partner, a sibling, a spouse, and go on this journey together. Make it a group effort, if you have a few good friends that are on the same path as you. You'll find out later how important it is to have others on this journey with you. You don't have to share your answers with them. Journaling is personal. But when it comes to brainstorming, coming up with new ideas, or thinking outside the box, you will find partners to be helpful. In addition, you have someone to cheerlead you along the way and keep you accountable to your goals.

Now that we have been introduced, good luck on your journey. I hope to see you at the end celebrating the victory. Know that this journey will take patience, diligence, and consistency. You didn't get to where you are in a day. So be patient with yourself, but also be honest. You'll be a different person at the end of this book and will appreciate who you've become in this journey. I am looking forward to celebrating your transformation!

Chapter One – The Mess

Do you know that moment? That moment when you look up from your check book or your online checking account and wonder how you got here? You look at the numbers and can't figure out where the road turned into a dirt path with more bumps, wash-outs, and deep potholes that could swallow you whole. I've been there. And to be honest, I've been there a few times.

For me, my mess started in college when I got my first credit card. It only had a $300 limit, so I really couldn't go crazy. And as a responsible student who graduated first in her class in high school, with Honors, and then will also graduate from college Suma cum laude, I was smart. I knew what I was doing. Every month, I would use the credit card to pay for things—especially when I would go out with friends. If I lost it, at least it wasn't my debit card, and with a low limit like that, no one could go crazy if they found it. Responsible, right? Right. Every month, I would pay that balance off. It was like clockwork. This is how you are SUPPOSED to use credit cards. And I will tell you, that system worked beautifully for a period of time.

Now, let's take a detour for the moment. Here's a fun fact: I am a triplet. Yes, as in an identical triplet. I have two sisters who look "just like me." What a way to grow up! I wish everyone could have the experience because it is so different from traditional siblings. They are A PART of me! I love them so much! It is unexplainable! But, I digress. The three of us are also the youngest of eight children. Yes, I said eight. Ha ha. Crazy, right? The five older children were just that, older. There is about a 15-year gap between us and the youngest. So, in college, I was also an aunt.

So picture this: It's Christmas time. I am home for the holiday and school break. I have purchased my Christmas presents for my triplet sisters, my parents, and my best friend. I'm all set. Wrong! I have a generous heart. I love my family so much! If I could give them the world, I would in a heartbeat. I find out one of my brothers has most likely gotten me a present. Now I feel like I should get him one. But, if I get him one, then I really need to get one for my other brothers and sisters. OK, how do I do this without going crazy? Good question, Angelica. Don't spend too much. We've all been here. Where suddenly there is this "obligation" to buy someone something, and Christmas time can sometimes create the worst of these situations.

Now, add into the equation that I am an aunt. Next, I feel like I should get something for the kids. Christmas is all about the kids! This leads to adding a few more presents to the mix. Christmas day comes. We all open our presents, thank yous and hugs all around. We eat Christmas dinner, and we all go home. Such great memories!!

Then January's credit card bill comes. I can't pay it in full like I normally do. I spent too much because instead of the $300, it was more like $500. You might be wondering, did I go over my limit?? Nope. Several months of on-time payments and what does the credit card company do? Raise your limit. Suddenly, I spent more than I could pay. At the time, I didn't adjust January's spending to have a lower bill in February, so I couldn't pay that bill off either. And that, ladies and gentleman, is what started my credit card whirlpool. I got sucked in, and I couldn't get out.

You have some story like that where you just got into a hole, and you couldn't get out. Years down the road, I had several credit cards that I still couldn't pay off even though I was paying over a thousand a month trying to pay them off. I couldn't figure out why I could never get out of debt. For me, it was two things. First, I was trying to pay off my cards incorrectly. Second, I was living outside of my means. I figured I would eventually catch up on the cards, so why not just pay with the card. It was so much easier to balance my checkbook that way. When I used the debit card to pay for everything, it was too much to keep track of in my checkbook. Then, when trying to balance my checkbook at the end of the month, it seems like so much more work. And that was the cycle I was stuck in for years. I couldn't get out of debt. It was a mess. A. MESS.

Now, we're going to take a look at your mess. You have to be as honest with yourself as I am being with you. I'm going to ask you some questions just to get to where it all might have started. We want to really get to the root of your mess. Let's start with some questions to jog your memory, and then just free write. Journal whatever comes to mind.

Can you remember the first time you had a hard time paying all of your bills? What was the root of the problem? Lack of income? Credit cards? Loss of a job? Overspending? What is your story?

Was it something you could have avoided, like my situation? Or was it unavoidable? What were your circumstances?

How did you feel at the time? I was confused. The numbers didn't seem to work correctly. I knew math, but the credit cards seemed to have funny math. What were your thoughts? Write it all out.

Finally, is there anything else you would like to say about your situation—your mess? Are you frustrated? Annoyed? About to give up? Get it all out. If it is taking up space in your mind, just write it here.

Great work! Amazing job! I know some of those questions may have been difficult. I am so proud of you for getting through the first chapter. Also, thank you for really being honest with yourself. That is what will make you successful in this process. This is just the beginning of your journey. Some of this will be fun. Some of this will be harder. But in the end, it will be worth it. You want to live a life of financial freedom, and I am going to help you on that journey.

Chapter Two – The Tools

Now that we've seen how you may have gotten where you are, let's look at some of what it will take to climb out of where you are now. The first thing you have to remember is that this will be a process. You will make mistakes. We all make mistakes when we're learning. However, we will also address how to handle those later. For now, we're going to look at what it will take for you go on this journey.

To start, what tools do you have so far? If you were going to climb a mountain, would you just hit the mountain with no preparation? Or would you make sure you had everything you needed first? Of course, you would be prepared! We will do the same sort of prep work here. Do you have a budget? Do you have a clear idea of what is coming in and what is going out? Do you work with a planner or advisor? Do you have an accountability buddy? These are all tools in your belt. You don't have to use them all, but it is good to know your options.

One of the first things I did was put together a budget on an excel spreadsheet. Income was at the top in one column; all of my expenses were listed in the next column in order that they were due. Some of the things listed were rent, car payment, cell phone, electric, and credit card. Income was listed by company (I have typically had more than one job because I prefer to have a lot of income). At the bottom, I saw a total of expenses and what was left of my income after expenses. It helped me plan for each pay check, what I needed to hold over each check if expenses one pay period were more than the income (like on the first of the month), and see where my money was going. It also helped me in those times when my income wasn't enough in a month to cover expenses (for instance, after I got divorced and a LOT of things changed). Then I would know how much more income I needed to make and what part-time job could cover that.

My sisters use a monthly calendar. They prefer to see it visually over the weeks versus my auto-calculated sheet. Income is written in green on the date it is deposited. Expenses are written in red on the dates they are due. Things like gas or food are added in at the time of purchase. Some people I've worked with like calendars with folders for the bills (this is seen less and less as we go more and more to paperless billing). What you have to remember is this: you are personalizing this to YOU. Ask yourself these questions: What would work best for me to use routinely? Is it too much of a hassle to go on my computer? Or am I always on it? Do I have a specific area where I pay my bills that I could keep my calendar? What is consistent about my routine when I take the time to pay my bills?

I also started working with a company part time that taught me a lot about money. I learned how to start investing, more about protecting my family, and how to get out of debt faster. I know there are several ways to get this information, but I needed help really getting on track and implementing some of these tools. Plus, what better way to learn something than to jump right in!? So remember, you may also need to get outside help too. There is nothing wrong with going to someone who knows more about a subject than you do. Maybe this is why you are reading this book right now. You know the importance of learning and studying. Now, let's see what you've been thinking during this chapter.

What tools, if any, have you used so far to figure out where your money is going?

____

____

____

____

____

____

____

What has worked for you in this process?

____

____

____

____

____

____

____

What hasn't worked in this process?

What are you willing to change to have a new tool work?

When you think of your income, what thoughts and feelings come up for you?

When you think of your expenses, what thoughts and feelings come up for you?

When you think of gathering your tools for this journey, what is going through your mind? What are you feeling? Are you ready to keep moving forward?

Finally, is there anything else you would like to say about your situation? Anything I didn't cover? Final thoughts for this chapter before moving on to the next step?

Again, another amazing job being honest with yourself!! You may add to this section or even review it as we keep moving forward. If you find certain tools don't work, don't feel like you need to keep them. Throw what doesn't work away and try something else. Keep what does work. We are all different, so what works for me, may not work for you. Remember, this is all for YOU to be successful. And for YOU to be successful, you will need to customize each area to you. I am here to guide you through the journey of journaling. When you really get how you think and feel about all of this, you will be able to let go, forgive, and move on to success!

Chapter Three – The Climb

Now that we have some tools in our belt, let's look at climbing out of this mess. Your journey will start with figuring out all of the details of your finances: where your money is going, how much your payments are, what interest rates are you paying, how much is going to food, how much is being spent in cash, how much is going to entertainment, what isn't being accounted for. This part of the climb is going to take time. Pull out a bank statement or print one from online so that you can see the payments—maybe even a couple months to see if there are variations. It may seem overwhelming, but this is going to be a foundation for all of the work we do later. Trust me. You will appreciate this all later! I promise.

Using whatever tool that works best for you, put in your sheet/calendar/notebook all of the information you have collected. You are going to start looking at this at least once a week to make sure bills are paid on time and money is available for all things when it is needed. You will track what you spend in cash also or on credit cards versus debit cards. You want to see where ALL of your money is going. Keep in mind, this may change month to month. You are creating a tracking system right now.

This will be a several month process, so each month you want to see if you overspent, where your money went, where you might be missing things. This is why I called this chapter The Climb. This whole process is a journey, but you are going to be learning new habits, thinking new thoughts, creating a new mindset. As you take this journey, know that there is an end goal—financial freedom! When you reach the end and have freedom in your finances, you'll look back and realize it was worth it! However, for now, let's keep climbing.

I choose to review monthly when I balance my checkbook. I like to keep track of what I owe and how much it's gone down, so I update those numbers at the end of each month. I love seeing that number go down! This is another way to feel like you are accomplishing your goals--when you see debt balances go down and savings balances go up. Right now, we're just talking about income and expenses, but part of your journey later will include growing your net worth. You can review this when you pay your major bills or at a time that works best for you. Try to do this review monthly though. This will help you understand the ebb and flow of your money and help you with your long-term planning for unexpected expenses.

One last thing before we do our journaling, some of these chapters are going to ask you to do work over several months. I would suggest you continue through the book as you take these actions. This journey is not a linear path. Instead see it as a spiral upwards. In a spiral, sometimes it will look like you are going backward, but in reality, you are still going up. Each chapter builds on the previous, but also may bring you back to previous concepts. That's ok. It's always good to review concepts, progress, and even mistakes. This helps us see how far we've come!

On this climb, what stood out to you most as you gathered all of this information?

Was there anything that surprised you during the month?

When you were using your tool to track everything (spreadsheet/ calendar/notebook, etc), how did you feel as you updated it?

When you started tracking cash or credit card expenses, what did you learn?

How did you feel about those transactions?

At the end of the month, are you spending more than you earn? What thoughts and feelings do you have when you look at those totals and where you've ended up?

Right now, what can you see that you can change monthly to stay on track or get on track?

Let's leave a section for month two of tracking. Write down any thoughts, feelings, ideas that come to you during the second month of tracking.

We'll leave one more section for month three as well. Write down any thoughts, feelings, ideas that come to you during the third month of tracking.

Because we are looking to change habits and mindsets, you want to have at least a 90-day commitment to your journey. After that, you will have started to develop new habits, new thoughts, a new financial outlook. Each 90-day commitment that you make will bring you even closer to your goal of financial freedom. Excellent job for really taking the time to make that climb!

Chapter Four – The Milestones

As you are journaling your way to financial freedom, we need to insert some milestones or goals. Without an end goal in mind, you won't have any direction. You need to know when you get off course and when you've finally reached your destination. This could look many different ways, so during this chapter, we will explore some of your options.

One of my first goals was becoming debt free. Depending on how much debt you have, this may seem overwhelming; however I can tell you consistency wins the game. Maybe each milestone is one of your debts, for instance, or a total amount paid off ($5,000, $10,000, etc). Another goal could be having $10,000 saved, then $50,000, then $100,000 and so on. It could be buying your first home or buying an engagement ring or even buying your first car (with no loan!). Financial freedom means so many things to so many different people that all of these could be part of it or none of them at all. This is where we'll do the work.

This chapter will be a little different because it will have sections of reading and journaling instead of one main chapter and questions. We need to get on paper your bigger goal first: Financial Freedom.

What does financial freedom mean to you?

Paint a picture of financial freedom. Write down what it "looks" like.

Once you have achieved this, how would you feel? What are some of your body sensations and emotions? Excitement? Worry? Tightness in your chest? Butterflies in your stomach?

When do you want to achieve this goal? Put some thought into this. Saying tomorrow isn't helpful unless you KNOW you are coming into a lot of money…tomorrow.

OK, now that we have a bigger picture, we need to create milestones between today and your end goal. Your milestones are going to be tailored to your own personal preferences. I am going to give you some examples, but you will work these out on your own. Just as I said earlier in the book, this is a process. You may get 30 days in or 60 days in and realize your milestones are too far apart. You may not get that sense of achievement soon enough to push through the rough patches. Or, on the flip side, you set them too close together, and you're hitting them all of the time making them seem less pertinent. Your structures will grow with you as you grow in this process. And remember, there is no "right" about any of this.

Let's start with a few examples. You could have a goal to have $1,000 or $2,000 in your savings account to start your first emergency fund. You could have an end goal of saving 20 percent of your income, but you may start at 5 percent or 10 percent. Each debt you have (credit cards, car loan, school loans) could be a separate goal or milestone. If you have children, a goal could be saving for their school, with dollar amounts attached to those milestones. If you own a home, you could have a goal to renovate without using credit. The sky is the limit here! Really focus again on what you want—what creates financial freedom FOR YOU and start to build those pictures.

In case you were wondering about the difference between a goal and a milestone…I guess it depends on perspective. For me, a goal is an ending, like paying off a mortgage. While a milestone for me would be a marker on the way to a goal, like saving $5,000 of a $20,000 down payment for a home. The only reason I bring that up is because you may want milestones on some of your goals.

Saying, I want to save $100,000 is a hard pill to swallow. But starting with $10,000 first seems much more achievable. OK, let's start looking at some of your goals.

When you think of savings or investments, what comes to mind? Thoughts? Feelings? Fears? Hopes?

____

____

____

____

____

____

____

What goals do you have for savings and investments? (Think high level for this question.)

____

____

____

____

____

____

____

What milestones can they be broken down into, if any?

When you think of debt, what comes to mind? Thoughts? Feelings? Fears? Hopes?

What goals do you have for debt? (Think high level for this question.)

What milestones can they be broken down into, if any?

When you think of property, what comes to mind? Thoughts? Feelings? Fears? Hopes?

What goals do you have for property? (Think high level for this question.)

What milestones can they be broken down into, if any?

When you think of providing for others, what comes to mind? Thoughts? Feelings? Fears? Hopes?

What goals do you have for providing for others? (Think high level for this question.)

What milestones can they be broken down into, if any?

Finally, is there any area I haven't covered? If so, list it here: ______________________________. What comes to mind when you think of it? Thoughts? Feelings? Fears? Hopes?

____

____

____

____

____

____

____

____

____

What goals do you have for that area? (Think high level for this question.)

____

____

____

____

____

____

____

What milestones can they be broken down into, if any?

I acknowledge you again for the work you are putting into this section! I know it was more than just journaling, but it will strengthen your financial mindset and financial foundation to have actionable goals. It may help you to organize these into a calendar or a notebook where you can have a timeline associated with the goals. You may want to create a visual tracker for some of the goals similar to the large thermometers fundraisers use to track donations. Remember, you can make this process fun too! This doesn't have to be all work and no play. Create functional structures for accountability to stay on track. This will be one of your keys to success.

What was your biggest financial slip or fall? How did it make you feel?

How did you recover? How long did it take?

What are some of the slips and falls you could see on your journey now? How can you prepare for future valleys?

When you get hit with the emotions of the valleys, how do you cope? Are you in the valley for a while? Or can you get yourself out of it quickly?

Even though this chapter is about the slips and falls, what are some of your highs during this journey? What great things have come your way?

Can these great things keep you pushing forward? How can you keep these in front of you to push you through your rough patches?

When you created your tools in Chapter Two, did you create tools to help you celebrate as well as track your progress? If you didn't, brainstorm now and write below ideas that you can use to celebrate your successes.

____

____

____

____

____

____

____

____

Finally, when you hit your bumps in the road or slip and fall, do you have someone you can call? Is there someone who can work this through with you?

____

____

____

____

____

____

____

I really want to commend you for making it so far into your journey. You are doing wonderful work! We've gone through several areas of how to reach financial freedom, and you have been so willing to do the work and be honest with yourself! This is how you will reach your goals. Each part is giving you different views, different perspectives, and different tools to get through your journey. When you hit one of those moments, come back and review this chapter. Look at your answers and remember how you planned on getting out of your valleys. When you wrote these answers, you weren't emotional. Use your unbiased thoughts to guide you through. You'll make it to the other side.

Chapter Six – The View

So far, we have covered the tools you may need, the slips and falls you may encounter, and the milestones you'll need along the way. On this point in your journey, I want to remind you that sometimes you need to stop and smell the roses, so to speak. If you were actually climbing a mountain, every so often, you would stop and enjoy the view. You would see how far you have come and take a moment to appreciate your new view from this new location. I am going to ask you to start putting this into practice for yourself. This could be at a milestone or just in a moment when you are feeling great about how far you've come. You decide when. Let's talk now about how.

To begin, we have to look at appreciation. Appreciation is defined by Merriam-Webster dictionary as "a feeling or expression of admiration, approval, or gratitude." You could have an appreciation for the job you have that gives you income. You could have an appreciation for the electricity that heats or cools your home. You could have an appreciation for the food you eat that gives you energy. Appreciation and gratitude can be felt along the way as you take this journey. One of the best changes in attitude I had was when I started appreciating what my "bills" gave me. Rent gave me a place to call home and a place to rest my head at night. My cell phone bill gave me a way to keep in touch with family and friends and a way to run my business. My internet bill allowed me access to a wealth of knowledge and a way to also share my own knowledge. My car payment gave me good transportation to see my community and see my clients. It was such an amazing way to view the bills I was paying. What service had they provided me that day? That week? That month? This is what appreciation can give you. It is another form of gratitude—a way to be thankful for what has been provided to you—a fresh perspective.

Along with appreciation, most people strive to make and earn more money. They want to be able to rent that apartment, buy that car, save for the home, yet many struggle with the idea that they deserve these things. I am here to tell you that you do deserve to earn money; you do deserve to save money, and you do deserve to have money. You were not meant to just make it so it could flow right out the door to your bills. You are meant to keep and accumulate money and wealth as well. You block your increased flow of abundance by not believing that you deserve it. Before moving on, let's do some journaling on what we've covered so far.

What does appreciation mean to you?

____

____

____

____

____

Right now, what do you appreciate about your life? Your income?

What do you appreciate about the bills that you pay?

Do you believe that you deserve to earn a good income?

Do you believe you deserve to save and accumulate money?

Do you believe that you deserve to have money?

Looking at your answers, can you see how there is more room for appreciation in your life? Sometimes we get worn down during our journey that we forget there are things we love about where our life is right now. You are about halfway through this book and this journey and this is the perfect time to stop and enjoy the view. Remember back to when you first started this book. Remember the moment you started reading it and where you were in your life at that moment. Now look to see how far you've come. We'll journal on it in a bit, but right now, close your eyes and see how far you've come. Take this moment to appreciate your journey thus far. Feel the feelings of appreciation, self-approval, and gratitude. FEEL them. Once you've captured fully those feelings, continue with your journaling.

Looking back at that moment, write down all that you remember from that moment.

What can you appreciate about your journey from then until now?

What is the biggest accomplishment thus far in your journey?

When you took the time to actually FEEL appreciation, self-approval, and gratitude, what other thoughts came to mind?

Are there any goals or milestones, actions or changes, or new habits you can add to your journey after gaining this new perspective and enjoying your "view"?

Thank you so much for taking this moment to really enjoy the view! How beautiful a vision we created! I know that you are willing to keep going, to continue on your journey. Moments like these will help you through times when you get frustrated or overwhelmed. Feel free to come back to this chapter and reread what you wrote about appreciation. Also, look at what your answers were to your last question. Add in those new structures to your daily and weekly plans.

Chapter Seven – The Partner

In the introduction, I suggested you have a partner or partners on this journey. If you have taken that advice, great! You may have gotten fresh ideas or perspectives from them or helped them get through a valley. You may have celebrated wins as well and had fun along the way! You have helped to keep each other accountable. If you haven't brought a partner along, this chapter gives you the opportunity to look into it further and add one to your journey, if so desired.

When you are taking on anything new, building a new habit, starting a new journey, it helps to have someone hold you accountable and work with you. Just as if you were joining a gym, having a workout partner helps make sure you get there even on those days where the bed seems so much more comfy than your gym clothes. We're using the same concept here. Again, I want to remind you that having a partner doesn't mean you need to share your journal with them. It just means you have someone to bounce ideas off of, someone who can help give you a fresh perspective, and someone to keep you on track. This could be your best friend, your significant other, a sibling, or someone who has expressed the same intention and goal as you.

When you have a partner, there are pros and cons. If both of you decide that you'll blow your budget to go on that Gotta Getaway Cruise, then you aren't using the partnership to your advantage. However, if you can keep each other focused until these concepts, thoughts, and actions become habits, you will benefit greatly. This chapter will give you some guidance on how to have a strong partner on this journey.

First, you'll want someone who is as committed as you are. Remember, this doesn't mean you both won't have your moments, but if you are both on the same level of commitment, you will help each other stay on track. Make sure they are willing to make changes financially, are willing to do the work laid out in this book, and are open to growing in this process. You may start this journey with five friends and finish with only two of them. That doesn't mean there is anything wrong with the three that didn't finish. It just means they weren't ready.

Second, you have to be honest with yourself and TELL on yourself. You and your partner will want to tell each other what you do to "get away" with your money cheats. If your weakness is shoe sales, let them know. If you can't stay away from watches, tell them. If cash in hand means you are eating out instead of saving it, plead guilty. When you can be truly honest with your partner, you can make sure you stay on track. My weakness used to be fast food, so when I had cash, I wanted to run through the drive-thru or grab quick food. I no longer have such a love for fast food because I prefer healthier choices now, but at the time, I just couldn't carry cash. Period.

Third, have some set way to check in on each other and update each other. This could be weekly calls, coffee meetings, email or text updates, or anything that best suits you both. I believe calls or in-person meetings are best because context can be lost in emails or text. In addition, when you have to say it out loud, it cements what you are learning. Talking it through can give you perspectives you would've missed by just mulling it over in your own mind. And, we all know, it's harder to hide when you have those weekly calls or meetings.

Finally, this may seem counterproductive, but you also want to be generous with yourself and each other. When you slip and fall, tell on yourself and get support from your partner. Your partner will do the same. The view you want to take is that this is a growing process. When you hit a bump, your partner is there to get you through it like you are for them. Your goal for each other is support, love, and encouragement. Don't beat yourself or your partner up. This is not a positive forward movement. Make sure you remember compassion and generosity through your journey. It goes a long way.

You know what is coming next: journaling. We want to get your mindset focused for what a partnership or accountability looks like. Also, I want you to see what partnership looks like to you.

If you have picked a partner(s), why did you choose him/her? If you haven't, who would you pick and why?

____

____

____

____

____

____

What does partnership look like to you?

What does accountability look like to you?

What are some of the "cheats" or downfalls your partner needs to know about you?

How do you feel about accountability and being held accountable?

Are you able to listen to advice with an open mind even if you don't agree?

Are you as committed to your partner's goals as you are your own? Are you willing to hold him/her accountable to those goals even if it is uncomfortable?

What is the best thing your partner can do to really encourage you when you need it? Make sure you tell him/her.

What is the worst thing your partner can do that would stop your progress? Make sure you tell him/her.

Brainstorm on ways you and your partner can hold each other accountable. Come up with structures, visuals, and timeframes for how you will help each other.

Fantastic job on completing another chapter! You have done your journaling, gotten your thoughts organized and out of your head, and you are able to see how partnership can help you on your journey. By answering these questions honestly and candidly, you have been able to get to some of your views about partnership and accountability. By seeing these, you will be able to see and handle any hiccups that may come. You may also see how your own parents' partnership (or lack thereof) may have impacted your views. We'll talk about that in the next chapter. For now, celebrate your work and progress on your journey! You deserve it!

Chapter Eight – The Little Child In Us All

It would be a disservice to you on this journey if we didn't talk about some of the influences of your own parents. When we're growing up, our parents' money views get ingrained into us, and we take them with us. This chapter will have you look at what you learned from your parents—whether you had one growing up or both, whether they stayed married, got divorced, or were widowed. Their money views have transferred to you, and you either live your life repeating their mistakes or live your life avoiding their mistakes. Either way, they have guided you.

The first thing I want you to remember is that your parent(s) learned from their parent(s). Nobody learned about money in school. It is passed down generation to generation. Savers learn to save. Spenders learn to spend. Habits are ingrained as you grow up. There is no right or wrong about this. It is what it is. Please remember that your parents did the best they could with the knowledge they had at the time. This is when you also bring compassion and generosity to them.

As you look at what you learned as a child, you will see where you have made choices that were based on that information. You may have had major successes from this information or you may have had major failures. Either way, we want to separate out what the little child in us thinks and feels. This may be something new for you, so just follow along with me.

We all have a little child in us that shows up when we feel afraid or angry or hurt. It could be a three year old or a five year old or an eight year old. Those emotions arise from some incident that made us first have those feelings: fear, anger, hurt, etc. For the purposes of this book, we just want to look at the little child who doesn't feel safe and secure. Financial freedom is all about security. You know you are taken care of and safe. We want to look at that.

We are looking at this just to see the views that could be in the background that you may have missed so far. These could be views that are tripping you up and you aren't even aware of them. They will be part of your existing money habits. When they are uncovered, we can make adjustments to the plan knowing these views/habits are in the background. The best way to explain this is how you tie your shoe. You tie your shoe the way your parents taught you. It hasn't changed your whole life, I would bet. You don't even think about it when you do it. You just tie your shoe. You have money habits that are this engrained in your life. You don't even think about them. It just happens, and you think nothing of it because you've "always done it that way." That is what we will address.

First, when you think of your parent(s) and money, what comes to mind? Are there pictures, feelings, stories? Write all of it down here.

____

____

____

Looking at these thoughts, can you see what you carried forward?

Reread what you wrote in the first journaling section of this chapter. What feelings and thoughts come up (about your parent(s))?

Did your parent(s) struggle with money? Or did they always have more than enough?

Are your money habits like your parent(s) or are they the opposite?

Close your eyes and picture yourself as a little child. When you see him/her and think about the word Money, what pictures, thoughts, and/or feelings coming to mind?

Do the same exercise and think of the word Safety. What pictures, thoughts, and/or feelings come to mind?

One more time, do the same exercise and think of the word Security. What pictures, thoughts, and/or feelings come to mind?

Finally, close your eyes and view yourself now, as an adult, in this exact moment in your journey, in your life, and think of Financial Freedom. What pictures, thoughts, and/or feelings come to mind?

What is different when you view these words as a child versus as an adult? Can you see any connections between the adult's view and the child's view?

____

____

____

____

____

____

____

____

____

You may see a connection where the adult you is trying to recreate the child's view of safety or security. You may also see some of the results of your childhood experiences magnified in adulthood. For example, your parents may have struggled to put food on the table, and you decided you would never worry about food, so you work extra hard to make a lot of money to make up for that experience. As another example, you may have seen credit used a lot growing up versus saving money for items, so you may have accumulated a lot of credit card debt because the credit got away from you.

There are many ways your childhood experiences have colored your choices now. I am not a psychologist, so I am not trying to analyze these experiences nor am I suggesting that you do. My goal here is to help you see what might be influencing your money decisions in the background. This way, you have access to forgive yourself for habits that are not serving you and let them go. You can learn new habits to help you stay on your journey to financial freedom. We know the end goal. We are just looking at all possibilities of slips and falls or detours in your journey. Catching them sooner helps you conquer them and get back on your journey to financial freedom.

Chapter Nine – The Affirmations

Throughout these chapters, you have been journaling on your thoughts and feelings and ideas that have been coming up during this journey. As you can see, a lot of your money habits have come from your money mindset. Our minds are powerful at creating and manifesting. However, we are typically letting our minds run on autopilot. On autopilot, your mind goes over past events, runs wild thinking about random possibilities during your day, fixates on negative outcomes, and creates a variety of scenarios, all in a matter of seconds.

Instead of letting it run amuck, what if you could use it as a laser pointer to shine on exactly what you want to create? What if you could feed it your goals and dreams? What if you could maximize the power of your mind? That is what we will cover in this chapter.

Affirmations are a way to feed your mind positive thoughts or phrases. They allow you to feed your mind very specific, concise pieces of information. I have used affirmations in a variety of ways throughout my life. I have written them on poster board and taped them up all over my apartment. I have written them out morning and night. I have repeated them out loud throughout my day. I have fallen asleep listening to them in my own voice. You can use affirmations in a variety of ways, but the most important is consistency.

First, let's look at some of the ways you can use affirmations. You can be creative and do what works best for you. Mix and match and see what you can create as a habit. You want your affirmations to become a part of you, your mind, and your daily conversation.

- Post the affirmations around your home, car, and work
- Write out your affirmation(s) in the morning and at night
- Repeat your affirmation out loud to yourself in the mirror
- Record yourself saying your affirmation(s) for at least 5 minutes and listen to it often
- Put your affirmation(s) on your vision board
- Put your affirmation(s) on your calendar or excel spreadsheet that you use to pay/track bills
- Create a picture and save your affirmation as your phone lock screen
- Create a picture of your affirmation(s) for your laptop/computer/phone wallpaper
- Before opening any bill or paying any bill, repeat your affirmation(s) out loud to the universe

These are just some ideas. Feel free to come up with your own or morph these suggestions into your own creation.

Next, we will look at some examples of affirmations. You want your affirmation to be in the present tense, state what you want, and be precise and concise. I will give you examples before you start to journal. Affirmations starting with "I am" are very powerful. "I am abundant." "I am successful." "I am healthy, wealthy, and wise." These are great to start your morning with, repeating in the mirror out loud to yourself. Seeing them in print will also reinforce it.

Surround yourself with your affirmations. Make sure you use as many of your senses as you can. Mix the forms of media so you are constantly reminded of them in a variety of ways to engage your mind. Also, keep them handy for when you have your moments of scarcity, upset, or overwhelm about money or bills. You can use them to bring your mind back to center. Here are examples for you.

- I am worthy of a very good income.
- I do not have to struggle to earn my income; it comes easily to me.
- Thank you Universe for all the good things in my life.
- I am open and receptive to new avenues of income.
- Everything is always working out for me.
- Money flows to me easily and effortlessly.
- Abundance is drawn to my every action.
- I am a magnet for Divine prosperity.
- I am ready to prosper beyond my wildest dreams. It's time!
- I am a magnet for enormous sums of money flowing to me.
- Money comes to me in expected and unexpected ways.
- People love to give me money because I add value to their lives.
- My income is rapidly increasing every day.
- I am healthy, wealthy, and wise.
- I am abundant beyond all measure.
- I am prosperous.
- All forms of opportunities come my way.
- I am successful at everything I do.

This just a start, but as you start creating the life and abundance you want, you'll craft more that are specific to you and your dreams. Also, some of these affirmations use words like Universe or Divine. You could also say God, Spirit, etc. Use whatever works for you and whatever fits your beliefs. I wanted to mix in a few so you could see how to write them for yourself. Finally, we move to journaling. This will allow you to really get into this chapter.

After reading all of these affirmations, how do you feel?

What are your top three affirmations that speak the most to you?

What are some of the ways you would put these affirmations in your life?

In those moments when you are struggling with money, can you see how these could help you? What are some of the ways you would use them to get out of a valley?

What are some of the ways you can use these to keep your mind positive?

When paying your bills, how will you keep these in front of you?

Looking at the examples of how to put these affirmations in your life, write down at least 3 of the ways you will put them into your life.

Use this section to create some of your own affirmations.

Finally, how do you feel after putting these structures into place?

We're ending this chapter on such a high note! Can you see how affirmations bring your mood up? That is exactly what we will be doing with these. Whenever you are struggling, come back to this chapter, read the affirmations out loud. Read every single one and BELIEVE it. If you are still on a rollercoaster, take three deep breaths, and read them again. You will get centered and back on track.

Chapter Ten – The Summit

If you haven't guessed it by now, there really is no Summit in this financial journey. There is no mountain top or end goal or final destination to Financial Freedom. You could feel financial freedom the moment your income is more than your expenses and you know what to do with that income. It could be the moment you pay off your last debt and know that all of that money is now going toward investments. It could be the moment you put the down payment on your first home. Financial Freedom is going to be a feeling you create, and this whole process, as you've learned, is all about your own mindset and emotions around money.

Throughout this journey, you have had your ups and downs, successes and failures, positives and negatives. What I didn't tell you at first is that those ups, successes, and positives are all financial freedom. It will be felt continuously throughout this process. You'll have moments where it doesn't feel so free, and you'll have moments where there is pure freedom. You'll know you've reached your "summit" when you can create more and more moments of pure financial freedom and less of those moments where you are struggling. That is the "end goal" in your journey with me: understand, know, and feel financial freedom as often as you can.

We're going to break this chapter up a little like we have done before because I want to bring you to that feeling of financial freedom. Journal on the following questions about your journey.

Think back on some of your successes during your journey. Write at least 3 of them here.

Looking back on these, how do they make you feel?

Now take a minute to think about financial freedom. At this point in your journey, what does that mean to you?

How does financial freedom make you feel?

What is similar between your successes and your view of financial freedom?

What is different between the two?

____

Now that we have written about both, take a step back and look at both. Can you see how you can feel financial freedom on a more regular basis? Can you see that financial freedom can actually be created by YOU on a daily basis? I want you to walk away from this time spent with me doing this work KNOWING you can create this feeling every day if you wanted to. It's really up to you. You could create financial freedom by knowing that you love your job and make your income doing something you enjoy. You can create financial freedom by taking the time to buy your favorite ice cream as a celebration for a job well done. You can create financial freedom when you pay your bills knowing you have a roof over your head, heat or air coming into your home, and a phone to call your loved ones whenever you would like.

Take time this chapter and really look at how you can create financial freedom daily in your life. Your journey has been practice for you. You have strengthened muscles, built habits, learned new things/ideas/concepts about money. You have expanded your tool belt in regards to money. You have changed your own financial wealth landscape. And if you feel like you haven't or you are having doubts, trust me, you have. Just keep going. Don't stop. We never see how far we've come during the journey. But you will thank yourself one year, five years, or ten years down the road for starting these changes now.

You've got the tools. Maybe you don't even realize how you've been using them. I am going to help you see what may be hidden. Let's get back to journaling.

In the last 24 hours, what occurrence/event/moment can you feel financial freedom about?

____

____

____

____

____

____

____

____

How about in the last week? Name at least three.

Going forward, what can you put in front of you (reminder, visual, phone alarm, etc) to focus on feeling financial freedom, abundance, and/or prosperity? (Hint, this goes very well with the feeling of gratitude also. What could you feel grateful for?)

Finally, so far in your journey, what has brought you pure Joy?

____

____

____

____

____

____

____

____

____

As we close this chapter, keep in mind all of these feelings and emotions I have been drawing out: abundance, prosperity, financial freedom, gratitude, and joy. The more you stay in these happy emotions, the more you draw the same to you. Like attracts like. We have done all of the work to bring up your emotional level and mindset around money. You can't be wealthy and stay stuck in the icky muck you started in. We've cleaned you up, helped you grow strong, and given you tools to stay on top. And when you slip, you climb out even faster than before. Your summit is feeling those daily.

Chapter Eleven – The Review

We are in the final chapter of our journey together. The final leg of our journey will be making sure you are prepared for the rest of your journey. As you may have guessed by now, this journey will be more than a few months or even a few years. Developing habits that lead you to Financial Freedom will be lifelong. In this chapter, I am making sure you are thinking long term.

In some of these chapters, I have talked about 30 days, 60 days, or 90 days. However, for you to really make this work, we are also going to have to review 6 months, 1 year, 18 months, 2 years, etc. In order for you to do this, you will need structures and reminders for review. For myself, one way to gauge progress was at the bottom of my budget excel sheet. I put the total debt I owed when I decided to put it all on paper. Then every so often, I would put a new date with a new total. Remember, it went down for a while there, especially the 9 months I focused on it. Then it went up when I had to get a new car. However, the overall intention was to have that number go down and get to zero.

You can also set specific dates to review, for example, at the end of June and December. This will help you see if you are starting to go back into some of your old habits or have extra money you can do something with. You can review when you get a raise, if it falls around the same time each year. Major life changes are also a good time to review—a new job, getting married, having a child, etc. Your goals may change over time, as well as your needs. All of these will cause changes in your plan. Don't expect to just go on autopilot. Remember, this is a journey.

To help, this chapter will focus on those times of review. You will not just be doing a number's check, like most financial reviews focus on. You will also be doing your journaling to see how far you've come. I've set aside those sections here for you.

6 Month Review – Date: ________________

How is your journey going so far? Name some of the slips or valleys you have had so far.

____

____

____

____

____

____

____

____

____

____

____

Name your successes and highs.

Are you able to stay on track with daily, weekly, and monthly habits for your financial journey?

How do you feel overall about your journey and how it is going?

What needs to be added to keep your mindset right on this journey?

What needs to be eliminated to stay on course?

How often are you experiencing true financial freedom?

What would it take to experience that more often?

1 Year Review – Date: _______________

How is your journey going so far? Name some of the slips or valleys you have had so far.

Name your successes and highs.

Are you able to stay on track with daily, weekly, and monthly habits for your financial journey?

How do you feel overall about your journey and how it is going?

What needs to be added to keep your mindset right on this journey?

What needs to be eliminated to stay on course?

How often are you experiencing true financial freedom?

What would it take to experience that more often?

Use these reviews as a way to keep what you've learned on your mind. We read books or articles often and then forget the information in a day, a week, or a month. This chapter will allow you a chance to get back into the money conversation. It will remind you of the end goal of Financial Freedom. If you feel the need to come back to the previous chapters to review a section, journal more on a topic, do that as often as needed. Some of you may even want to get a second journal of blank pages to just write down your thoughts on a daily basis. Journaling is a great way for you to get all of that mess out of your head so you can think more clearly. It may help you in other areas of your life as well. I wouldn't have been called to write this book if I didn't feel so strongly about the benefits of journaling.

What an amazing job you have done by staying the course long term! I am so impressed with your tenacity and endurance!! And I am so very proud of you! Financial freedom is yours! Thank you for enduring this process and climbing that mountain.

Conclusion

Thank you, thank you, thank you for taking this journey with me. I hope that you have learned a lot about yourself and your thoughts and feelings about money along the way. There is so much more I could teach you about the intricate details of budgets and money, investing and financial education. However, this book was really meant to get your mindset right around money. There are so many books out there on all those intricate details, and I believe that a major component has been missing this whole time. That missing component is this journey: understanding how you view money, your money mindset, hidden habits you created with money, how you grew up around money, and those thoughts associated with money. That is what this journey is meant to have unfold for you.

I am so grateful that you have completed this book and worked with me. I am so grateful that you have really focused and done the work to get to the end of this journal. I know that as you're reading this, there are portions of this book that you'll have to come back to at a later time, and I really hope that you take those steps and put those reminders in place to do so. Your journey is a process, and you'll be learning along the way. As your income increases and increases and abundance flows to you more naturally, your views and goals will change. I hope that this book is the catalyst that brings more abundance and more prosperity your way so you experience true financial freedom continuously. I hope that you've used this book to really clear out some of those thoughts that are not serving your future goals and dreams.

To close out our journey, I will tell you how this book has helped me. I have been able to process my own journey to financial freedom as I put these words onto paper. The answers to these questions have poured out of me as I ask them to you. Even though this book has come from doing this work already, writing this has allowed even more closure to some of the financial valleys I have gone through. As I have guided you, I have seen my own peaks and valleys flash before my eyes. Therefore, I want to thank you for truly taking this journey WITH me. If this book hadn't been called forth because you needed and wanted this information, I wouldn't have had the experience of this journey either.

With love and gratitude, I thank you. I wish you all of the abundance and prosperity you could ever hope for. And finally, I send you pure love and joy as you continue to feel true financial freedom.

Made in the USA
Monee, IL
08 November 2026

67383849R00069